ROCK STUDIES

for DRUMSET by James Morton

Online Audio www.melbay.com/94379BCDEB

AUDIO CONTENTS

1	Chart 1 [3:39]	11	Chart 6 [2:48]
2	Solo 1 [3:43]	12	Solo 6 [2:51]
3	Chart 2 [2:04]	13	Chart 7 [2:58]
4	Solo 2 [2:03]	14	Solo 7 [2:57]
5	Chart 3 [2:25]	15	Chart 8 [1:59]
6	Solo 3 [2:24]	16	Solo 8 [2:00]
7	Chart 4 [2:27]	17	Chart 9 [2:31]
8	Solo 4 [2:26]	18	Solo 9 [2:30]
9	Chart 5 [4:36]	19	Chart 10 [2:44]
10	Solo 5 [4:36]	20	Solo 10 [2:46]

I0805600

MEL BAY

1 2 3 4 5 6 7 8 9 0

Visit us on the Web at http://www.melbay.com — E-mail us at email@melbay.com

Contents

Introduction

Today, a serious rock drummer needs to be as competent a player as any other musician, and with that goes the knowledge and ability to play in different styles. There is an obvious benefit to being versatile: You are able to play with more people in different situations. A recent example of this is drummer Greg Bissonette. I had known Greg as the drummer for Maynard Ferguson's big band, and here he was in a new gig, playing with David Lee Roth. What a switch! In the long run, the versatile drummers tend to gig more.

Another benefit of being versatile is that your playing becomes well rounded. The creative drummers that come up with new and exciting patterns (just when you thought you've heard it all) are those who have studied other styles of music. The '60s music of Jimi Hendrix was made much more interesting with the jazz-flavored rock drumming of Mitch Mitchell. Today, almost all rock drummers who have any lasting influence seem to be musicians who are aware of all styles which could influence their music.

This book is not intended for beginners, although I think beginners could benefit from it. You can approach this material at whatever level you are. There are ten charts here, each representative of a rock style that you will encounter as you progress as a musician. Some are simple in structure, others are rather complex. I urge you to take each one seriously, as that is what a serious musician would do. Each chart is preceded by an introduction and a listing of the key measures with suggested stickings. Study these before going on to the chart. It will help you through the tricky passages.

When you look at the chart, check out the form of the piece before you play it. Be aware of all the repeats, first and second endings, codas, etc. Play through the chart slowly before playing with the recording. Each chart on the recording is presented twice: full band mix, and band mix without drums.

Speaking of the recording, this book is indispensable without it. On it, you will get a chance to hear the terrific musician performing with me on the recording: Mike Keneally, a guitarist known for his work with Frank Zappa, among others. Mike is a good friend as well as an outstanding musician, and I appreciate his help in preparing the recording.

Happy drumming,

James Morton

Legend of Notation

All the charts in this book use this legend of notation:

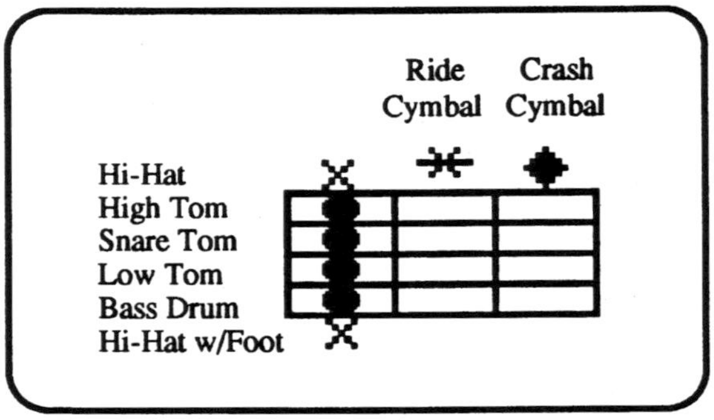

Introduction to Chart One

Chart One is in the style that is probably the most dominant in rock: **straight eighth-note rock.** The introduction is a spare bass-drum quarter-note line, with hi-hat backbeats added after the first four measures. This "bare-bones" beginning makes the fill and entrance at *A* much more dramatic. This is a very pulse-oriented piece, so the bass drum maintains the quarter-note drive throughout the chart. Note that the only difference between *A* and *B*, apart from the fills, is the open hi-hat that is initiated at *B*. During the breaks at *C*, the bass drum is still moving along. *D* is a recap of *A*.

Suggested Stickings

All the fills in Chart One are based on two sixteenth notes going into a third note. These three-note groupings should be played with a RLR sticking whenever they occur.

Measure 8

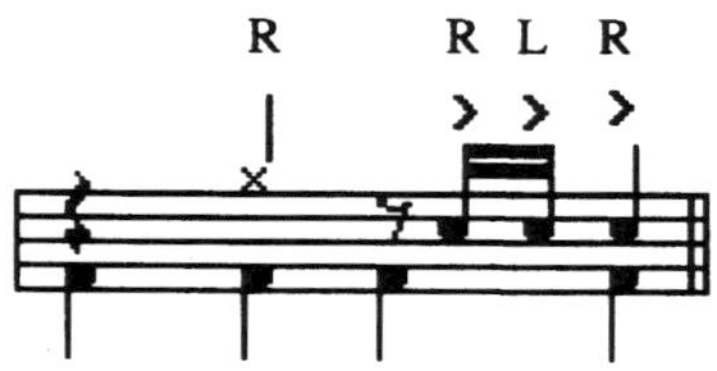

B, Measure 8

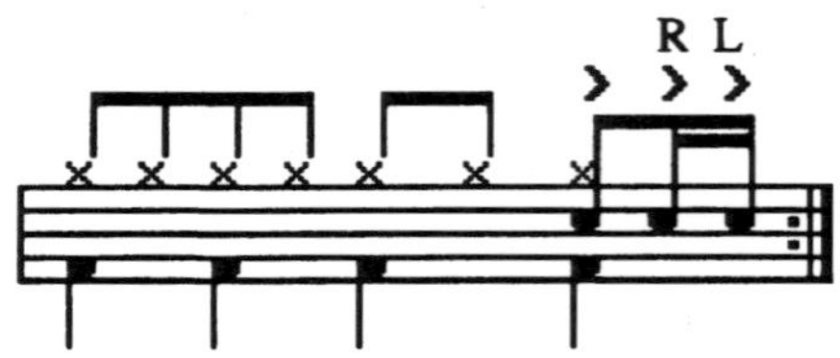

C, Measures 1–8

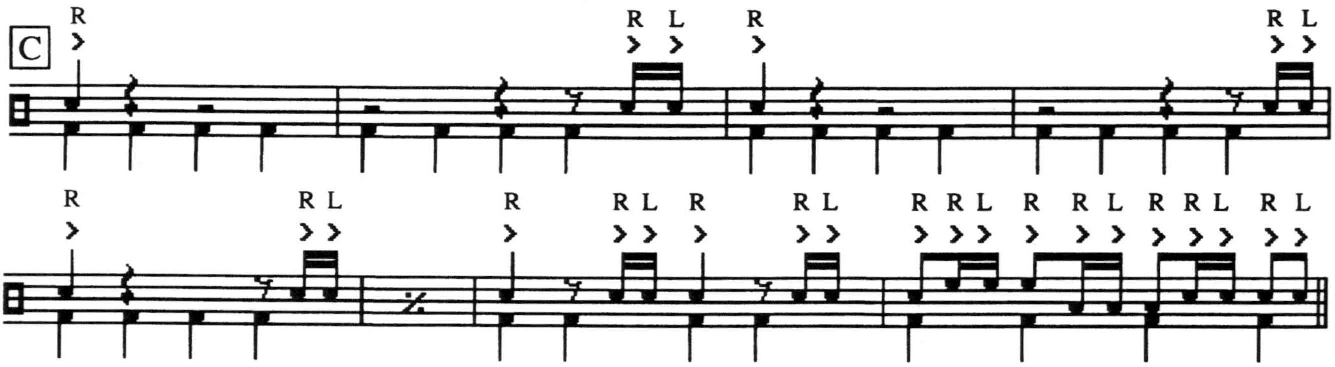

Chart One

Eighth-Note Rock

Practice Tips

- The best practice is the practice you do!
- Slow and correct are better than fast and wrong.
- If you can't do everything, do something. Everything else will follow.
- If you can count it, you can play it.
- Set reasonable goals for yourself. Don't tell yourself you will practice for eight hours and then not do it. Try for one hour and see how you go from there.
- Never play tight. Always play loose and relaxed. Strive toward a smooth and flowing feel.
- Practice with a metronome. It will enhance your precision and show you where your tendencies to rush or drag are.

Introduction to Chart Two

Chart Two, like Chart One, is another **eighth-note rock song,** but this time with **more fills,** and an interesting **"linear"** time-keeping pattern at *B*. Note the use of **flams** in the second ending and also in the next-to-the-last measure. It is a good idea, when playing fills, not to think of the fills as substantially different from the beats you are playing. Rather, try to view the fills as a continuation of the time. When played in this perspective, beats and fills tend to be played with a smoother transition.

Suggested Stickings

Measure 4

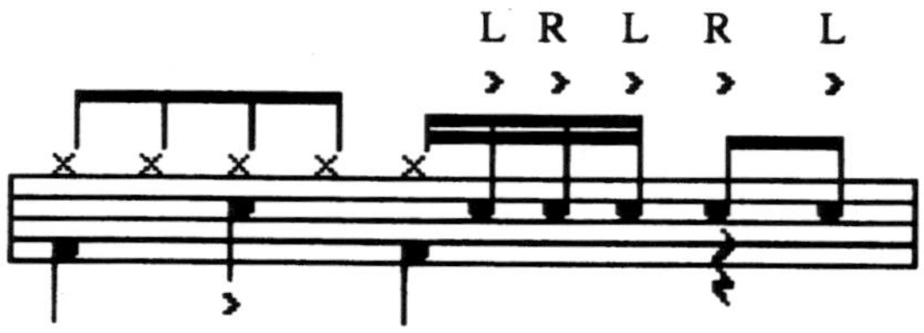

Measure 8

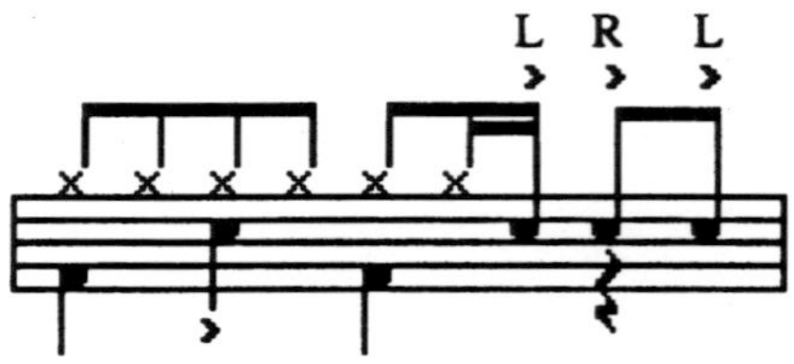

A, Second Ending

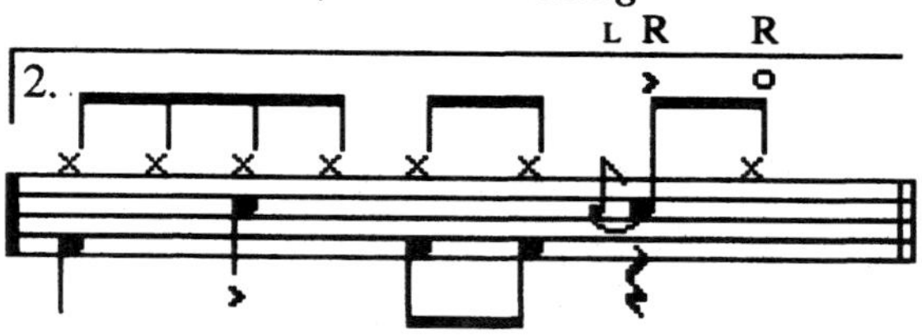

B, Measures 1–14

C, Measure 4

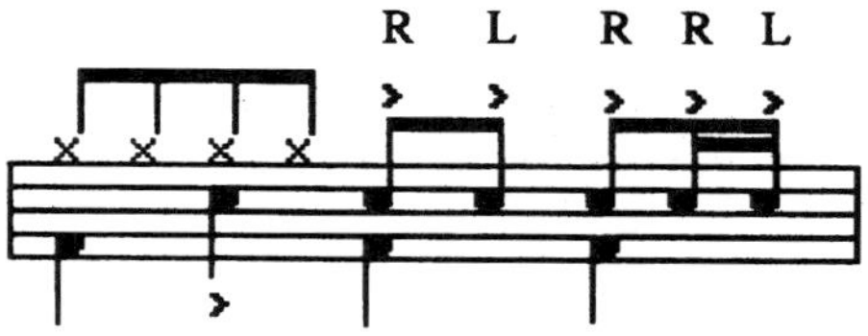

C, Measure 8

C, Measure 12

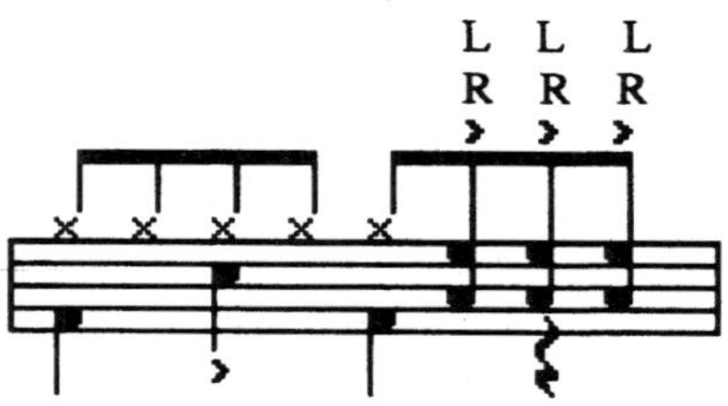

C, Measure 16

Chart Two

Eighth-Note Rock

Introduction to Chart Three

In Chart Three, we take a look at a combination of styles: eighth-note rock and country. Rhythmically, **country rock** and eighth-note rock are pretty much the same. A country flavor can be added by adding a rim click in place of the snare backbeat. I wrote this chart with such country rock groups of the '70s as the Eagles in mind. Strive to create a consistent sound on all voices of your drum set, especially the rim click. The form of this chart, after the intro in the first line, is **AABABA,** a fairly common songwriting formula. See if you can recognize the changes. A good drummer should also have a good ear.

Suggested Stickings

At *C* and *E,* play the two sixteenth notes with a RL sticking, even though you are playing a right-hand ride pattern throughout. This will allow you to play the accents in an unforced way. To make the accents stand out, play them against the hi-hat cymbals at an angle, while playing the ride pattern "on top" of the hi-hat. This will create a nice contrast of sounds. Watch the transition from *C* to *D.* At the last measure of *C,* play the two accented snare notes with the butt end of the drumstick, and then position your left hand as smoothly as possible into playing the rim click which follows. The same transition takes place from *E* to *F.*

C and E, Measures 1–7

Chart Three

Country Rock

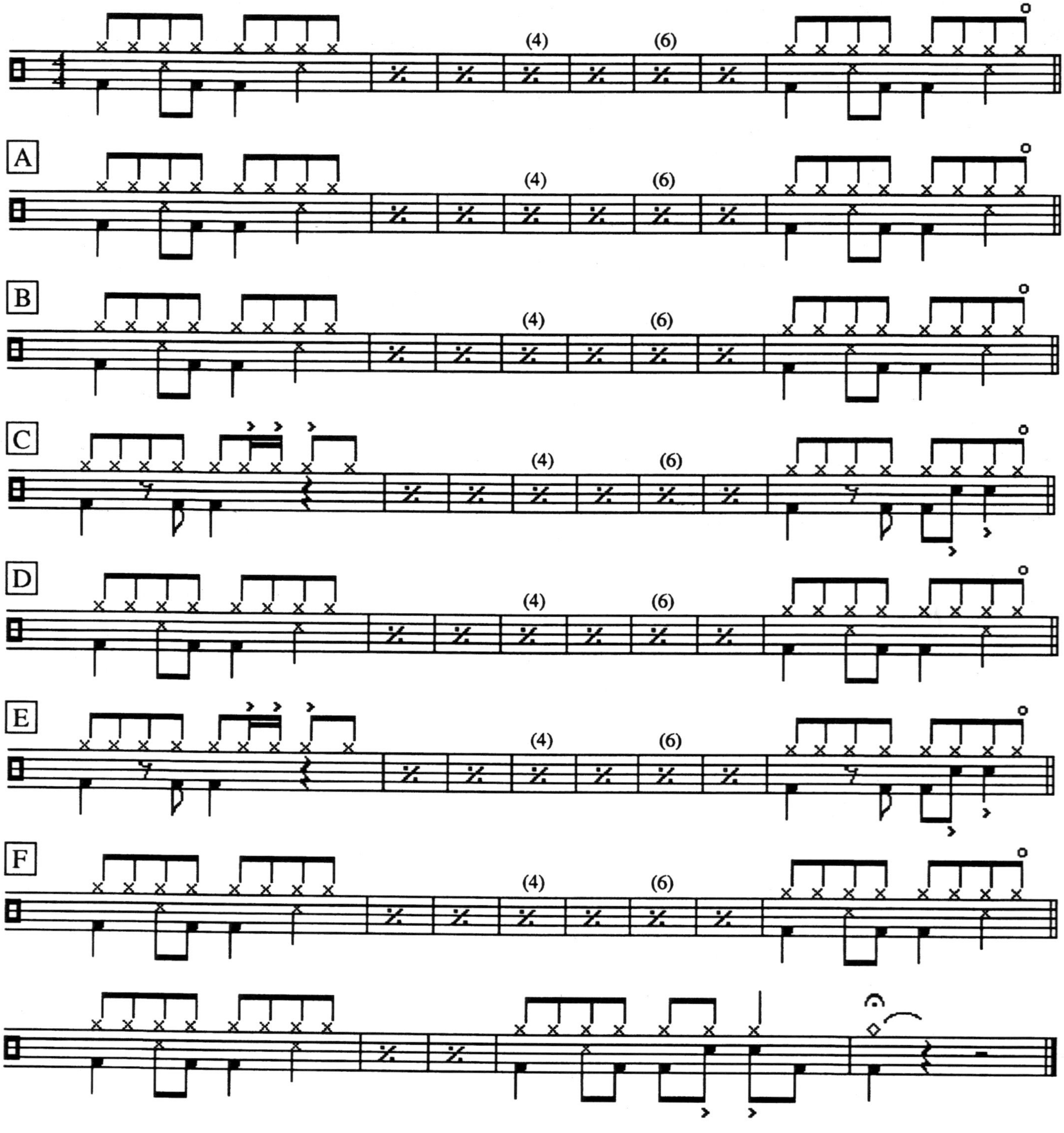

Introduction to Chart Four

Chart Four is in a **sixteenth-note rock style,** with the ride patterns played **hand to hand** (RLRL). Although many rock bands utilize this style, the drumming of Larry Mullen of U2 comes to mind here. Note that the bass drum keeps a quarter-note pulse throughout (except the last measure).

Suggested Stickings

Because the hi-hat pattern is played hand to hand (RLRL), the backbeat and short fills are derived from that sticking, as the following measures indicate.

Measure 8

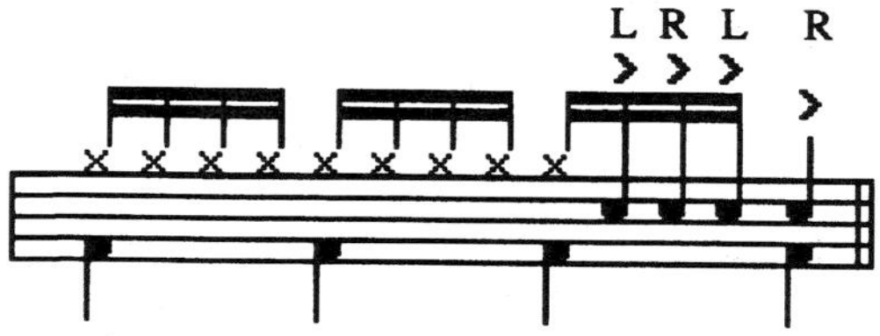

A, Measure 8

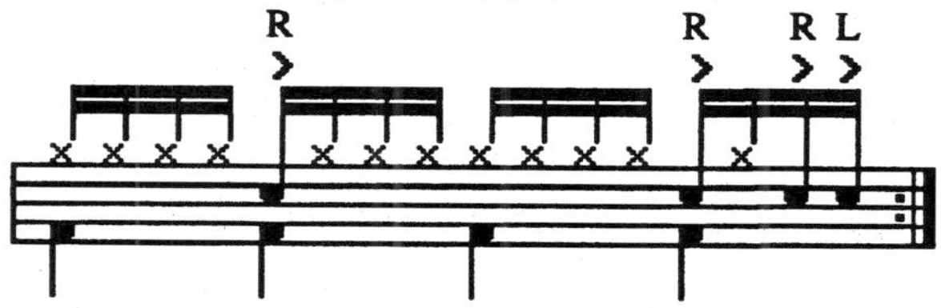

B, Measures 2, 4, 6, 8

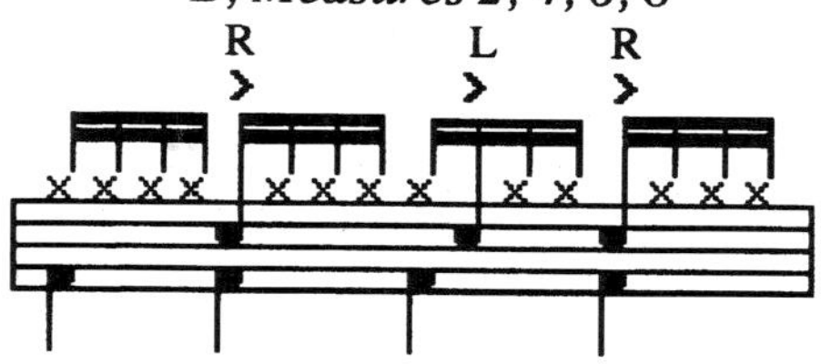

C, Measures 1–7

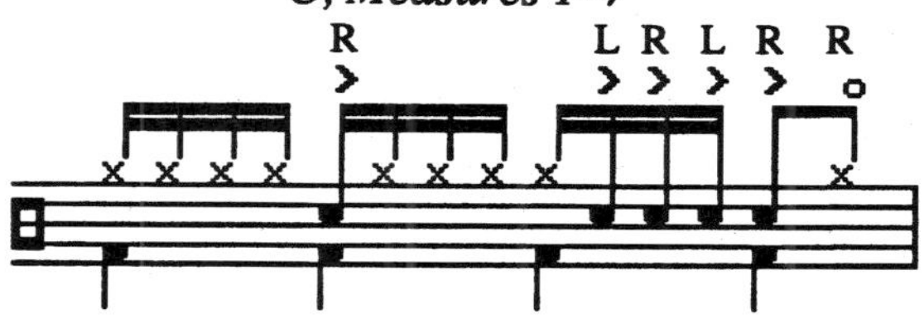

Two-Measure Pattern at Coda

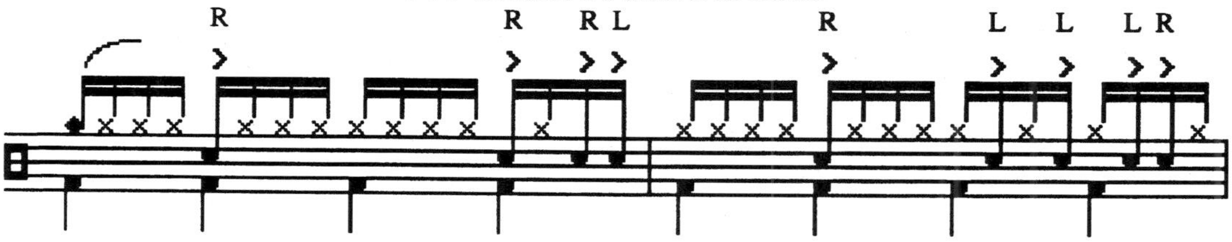

In the examples above, when both hands are coming off the hi-hat to the snare with a lot of interaction, be careful that the sticks don't hit each other inadvertently. Work out a smooth "flight pattern" for each exercise, and perhaps adjust your hand positions accordingly. You should also have plenty of clearance between the snare drum and hi-hat.

C, Measure 8

Coda, Measure 8

Chart Four

Sixteenth-Note Rock

Introduction to Chart Five

Chart Five is a **moderately slow piece with a sixteenth-note feel.** As the extended rest at the beginning indicates, you enter on the fifth measure. Take care that you follow the repeats as indicated. When I have to sightread a chart, the first thing I look at is the form of the piece, with all the repeats. I do this because, if I miss the repeats, it won't matter if the notes are correct!

Suggested Stickings

Measure Before B

First Ending

Second Ending

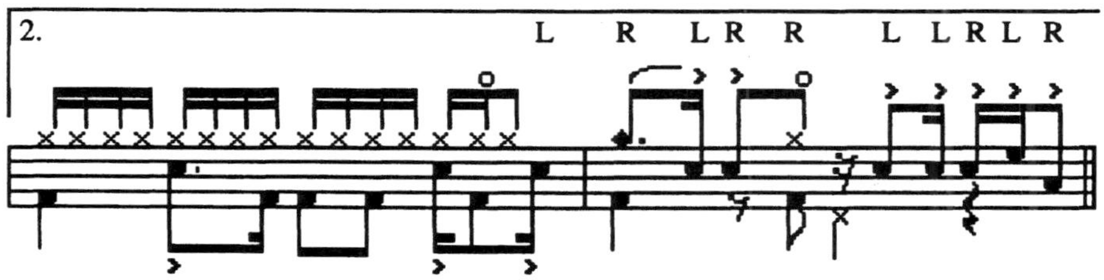

C, Measure 8

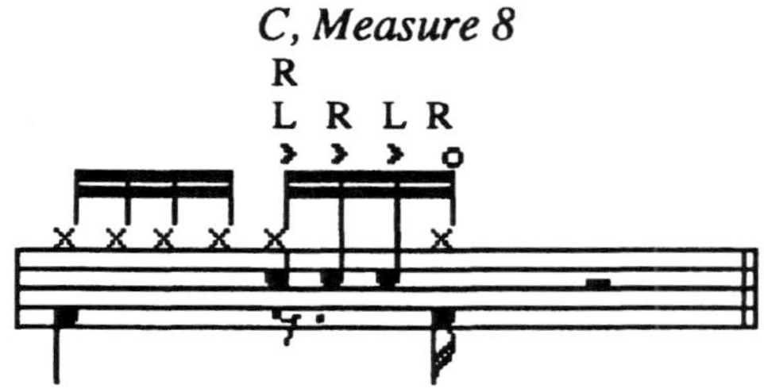

Coda, Measures 1–2

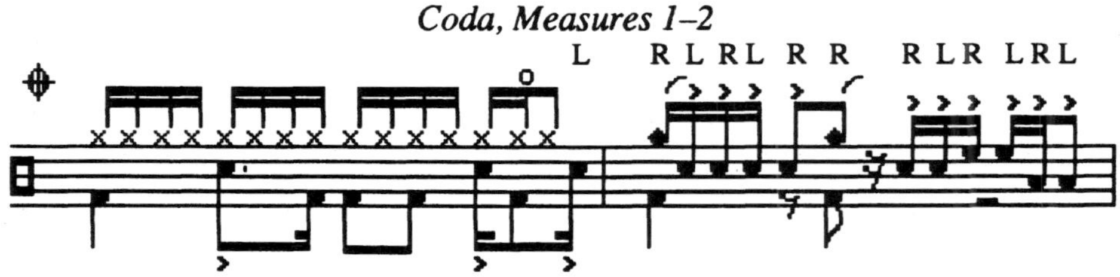

Chart Five

Slow Sixteenth-Note Rock

Introduction to Chart Six

Funk music has always been a favorite style of mine. The syncopated rhythms and the "up-front" bass lines really bring out the rhythm section of a band. While it is always important to be tight with the bass player, it is especially important in funk music. For some historical perspective and inspiration, listen to anything James Brown did in the '60s. Tower of Power's recordings with drummer David Garibaldi in the '70s are still the model of funk for many drummers.

At *C,* you have a chance to let loose with some solo spots. You may want to practice different solo ideas before playing with the recording, where I play a solo only on the full band track. On the other version (band track without drums), you are free to play your own solos. On the following page, there are some solo ideas, as well as a transcription of the solo I play. Try them all out, and then make up your own. Be sure to stay in time while you solo. Many drummers rush spots like this.

Suggested Stickings

Note that both fills employ a **paradiddle** sticking.

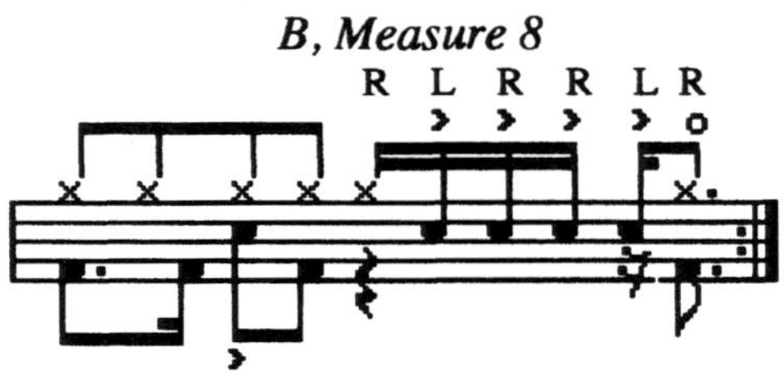

Solo Ideas for Chart Six

1.

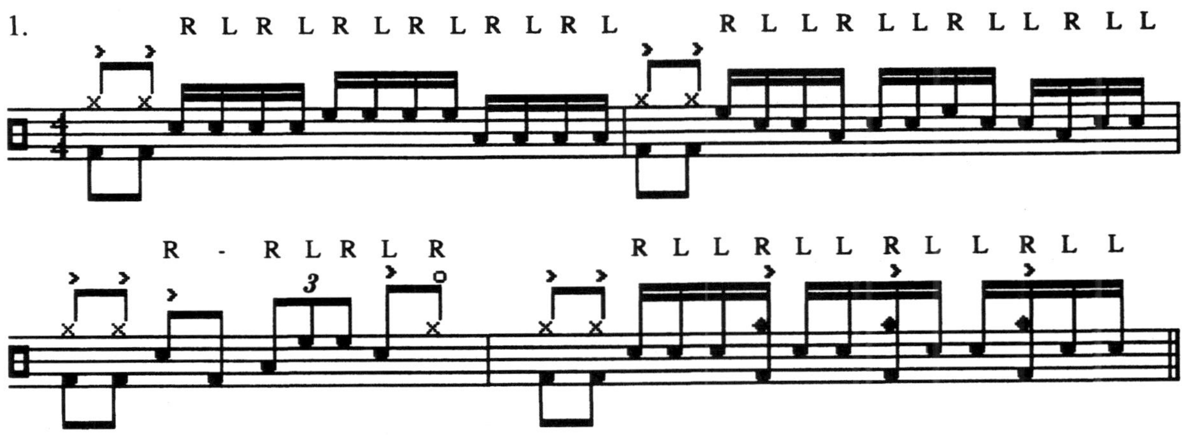

2.

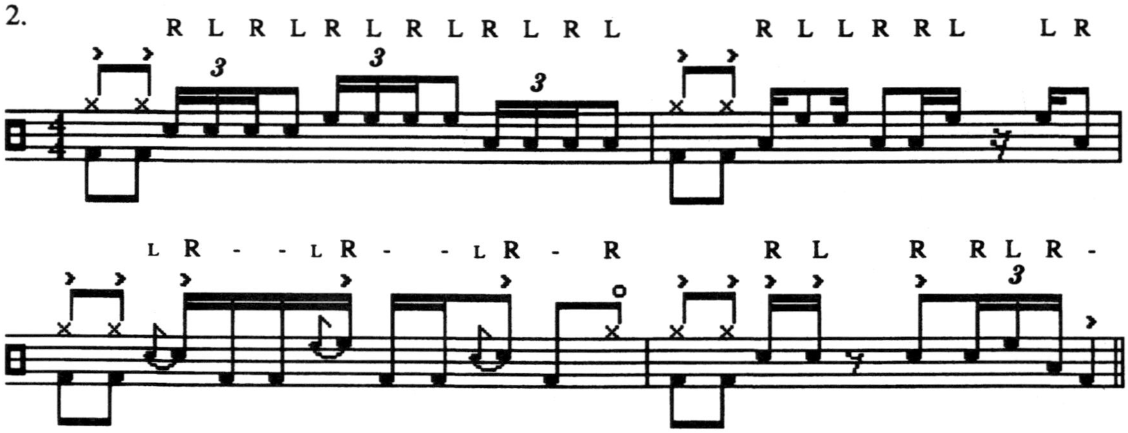

3. (This solo is performed on the recording.)

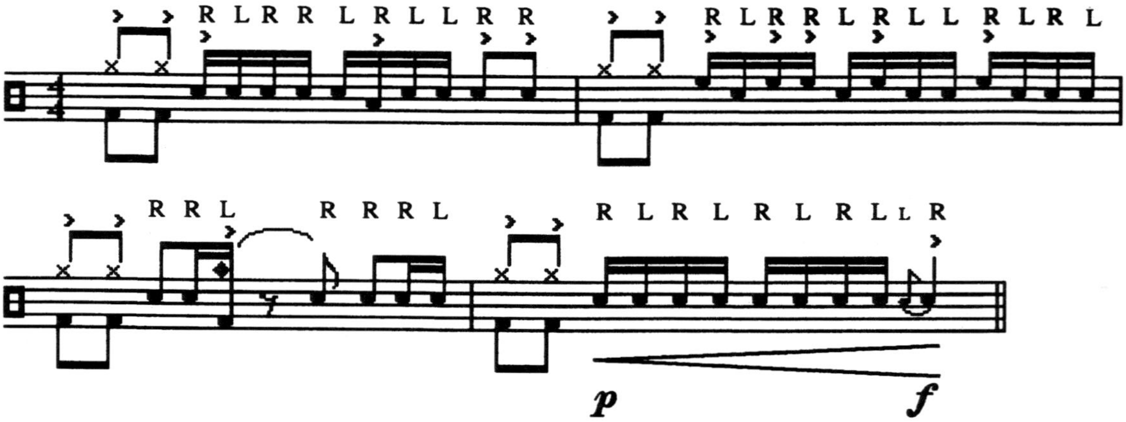

Chart Six

Funk

Introduction to Chart Seven

Chart Seven is a **triplet blues ballad** — sort of a cross between Toto's "Hold the Line" and Walter Egan's "Magnet and Steel." **Both verse and chorus utilize a two-measure pattern,** with the ride pattern on the hi-hat on the verse *(A),* then on the ride cymbal on the chorus *(B).* At *B,* the hi-hat is pedaled on beats 2 and 4, and this creates a **hemiola** effect when you play the **quarter-note triplets.** If you have trouble playing this, try counting all triplet counts, whether you play them or not.

Suggested Stickings

Intro Fill

A, Measure 8

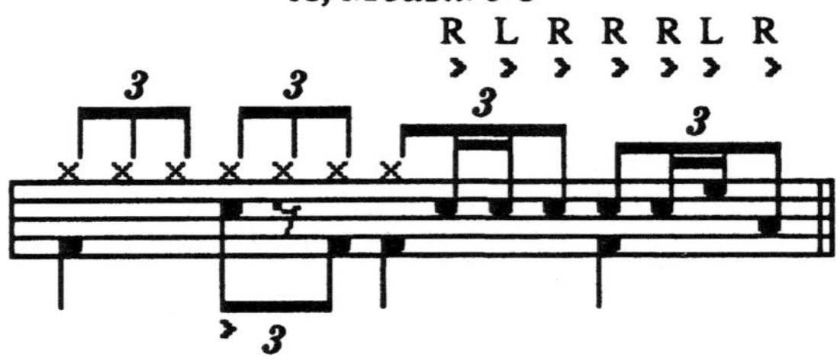

B, Second Ending

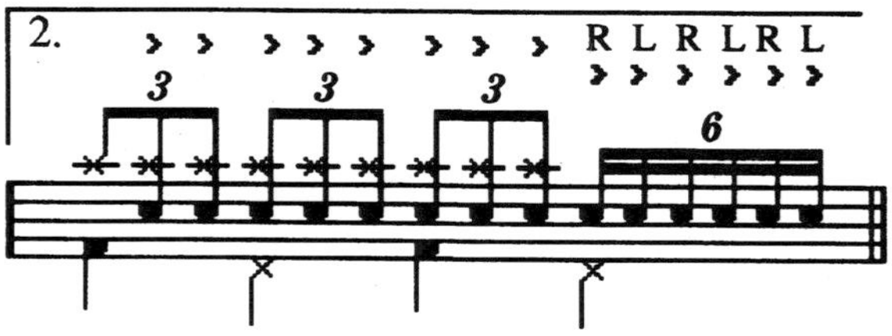

C, Measure 4

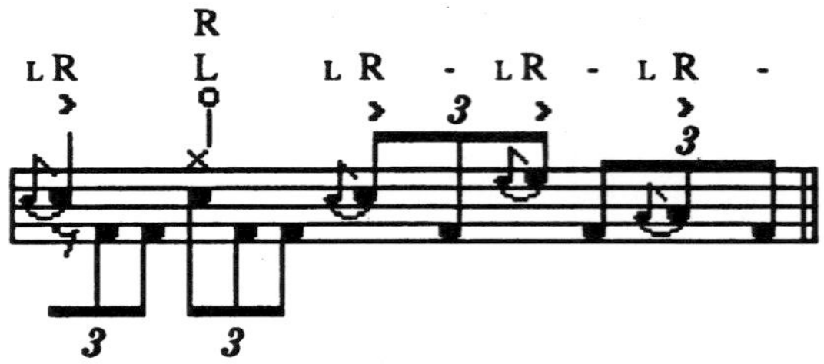

D, Measure 6

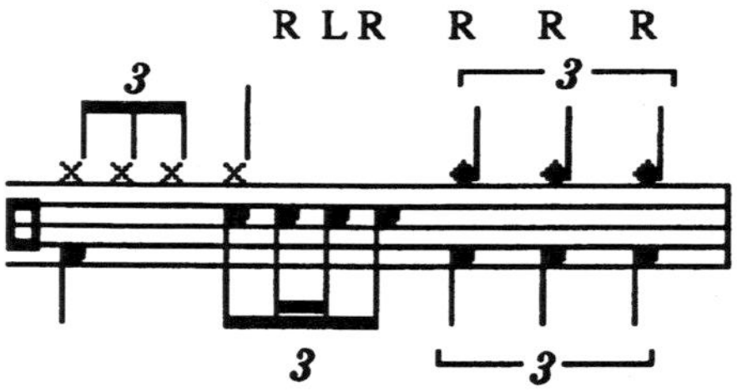

Chart Seven

Triplet Blues

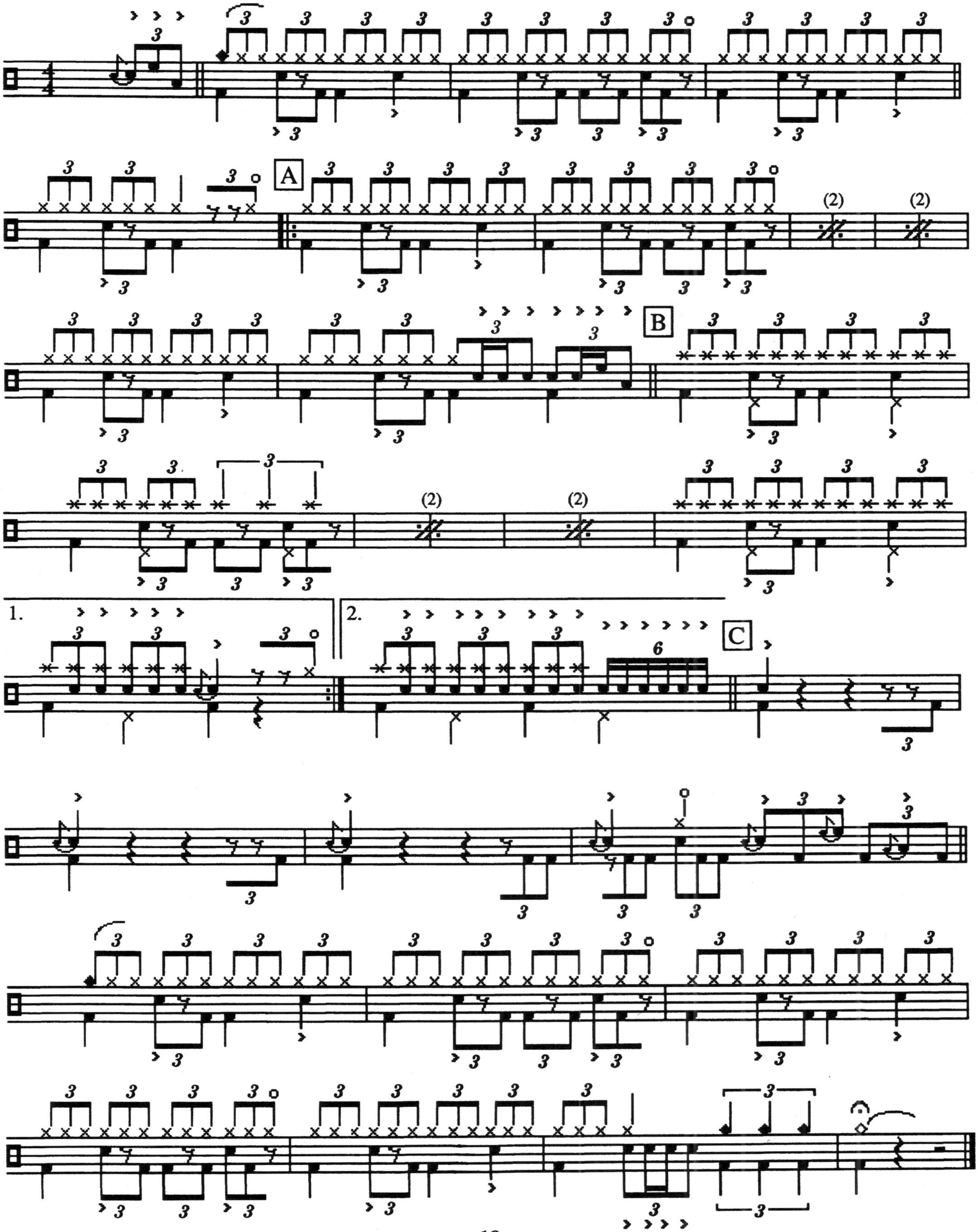

Introduction to Chart Eight

Chart Eight is an **uptempo,** high-energy rocker. The **quarter-note ride pattern** creates a driving pulse and makes the tempo accessible. After the eight-bar intro, *A* gives us the primary theme. The four hi-hat quarter notes at the end of *A* are a transition to a different feel at *B*. With the snare on the third beat, *B* has a **half-time feel.** Note, however, that the tempo remains constant. *A* and *B* repeat, and that brings us to *C*, which takes us out.

Suggested Stickings

Measure 8

A, Measures 13–14

C, Measures 2, 4, 6

Chart Eight

Uptempo Rock

(2)
(2)
(2)
B
Half-time feel
C

Introduction to Chart Nine

Chart Nine is a moderate shuffle that should be played with some degree of subtlety. Play the hi-hat nice and tight and the backbeat crisp. There are two offbeat breaks that should be played with precision: the last measure of the fourth line and the next-to-the-last measure of the sixth line. The feel I had in mind when I wrote this chart was along the lines of Steely Dan and/or Paul Simon. Both artists were renown for using top studio drummers. Watch the D.S. at the end of the sixth line.

Suggested Stickings

Measure 8

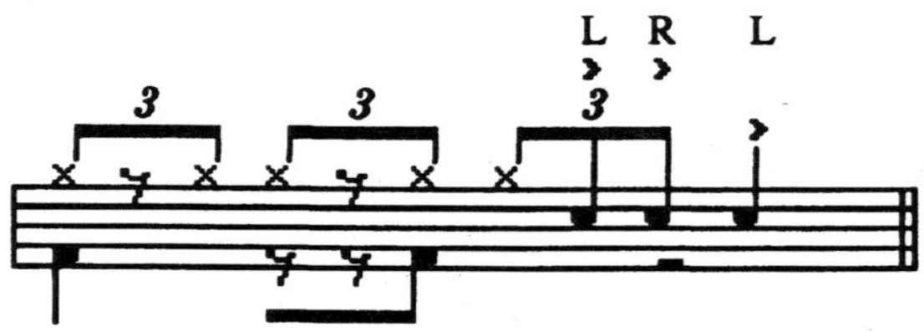

Line 6, Measures 3–4

Chart Nine

Moderate Shuffle

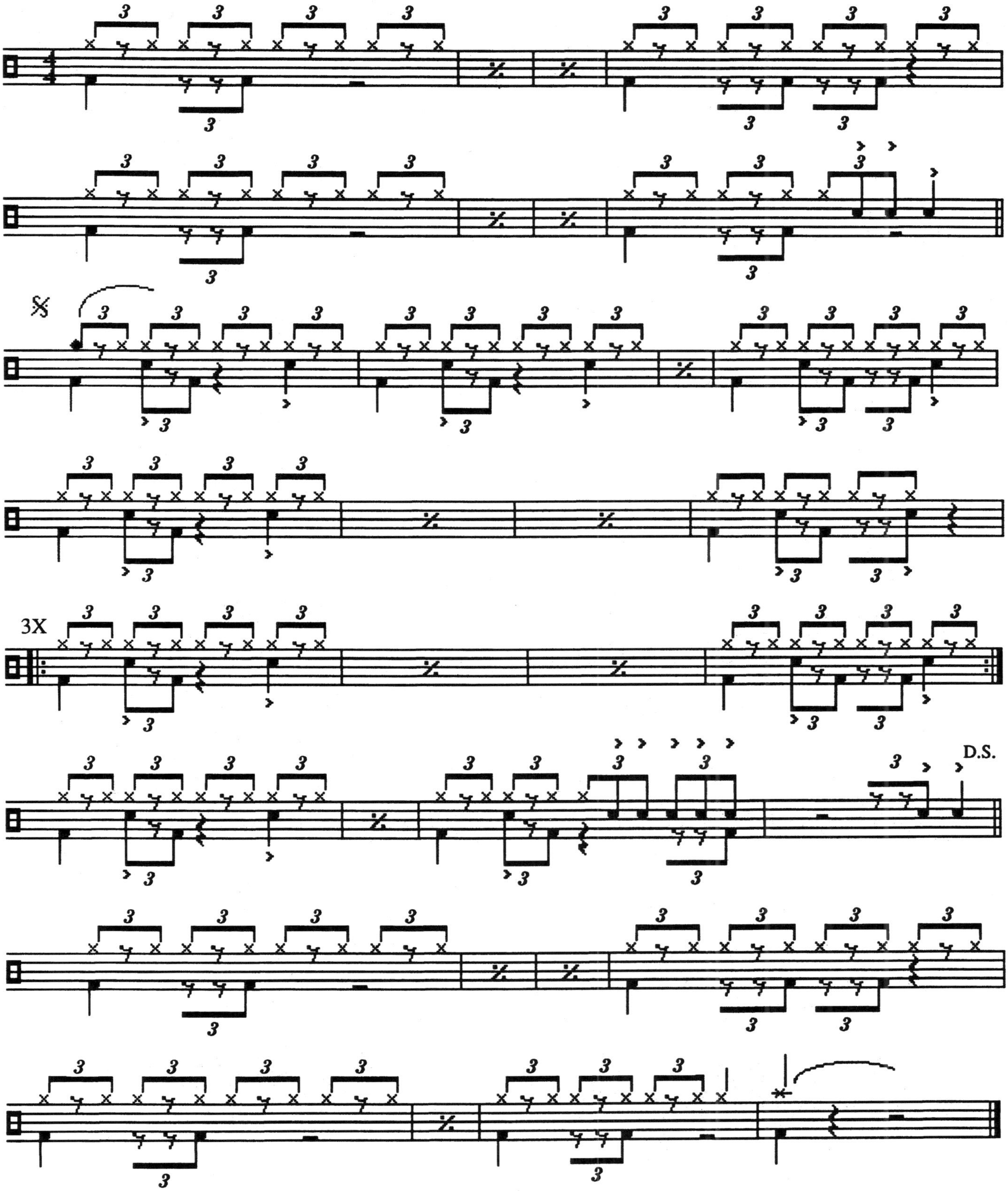

Introduction to Chart Ten

Our last chart, Chart Ten, is perhaps the most ambitious. There are some technically demanding situations throughout, and I urge you to take out of context those measures that trouble you and practice them slowly until the necessary reflexes become automatic. To play a hard-rock style like this, each note should be solidly hit. Terry Bozzio and Neil Peart come to mind as two drummers whose fills are very solid and clean. All the fills that have thirty-second notes are to be played with single strokes, as single strokes give the definition and punch that are required. During the quarter rests, it might be helpful to keep the eighth-note count going in your mind to hold your place.

Suggested Stickings

Measure 4

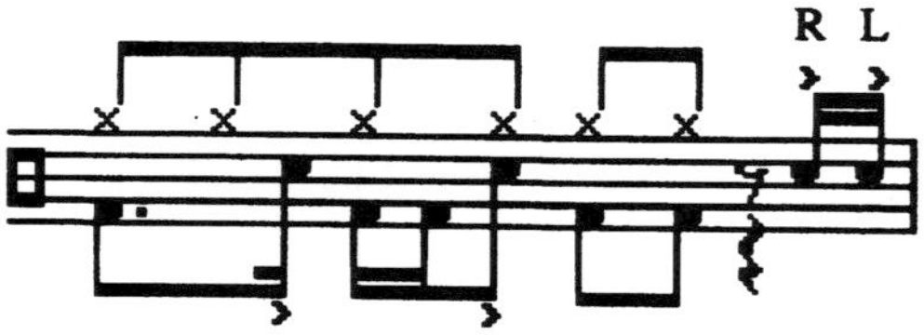

Measure 12

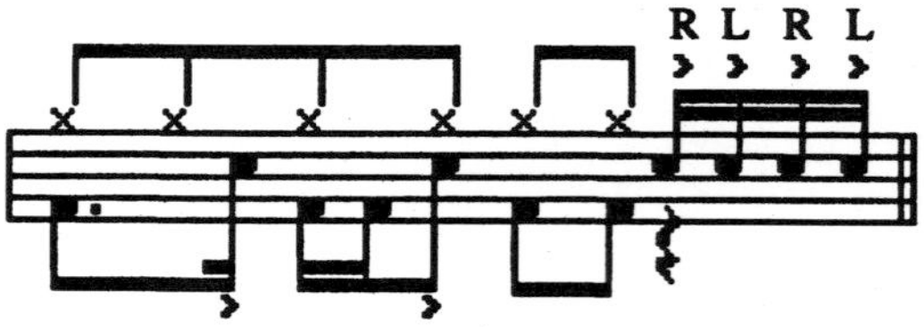

Measures 13–14

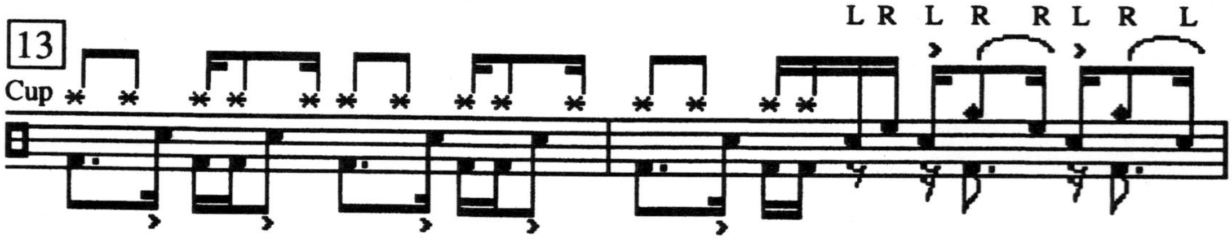

Measures 17–19

Measure 20 (First Ending)

Measure 21 (Second Ending)

Measure 25

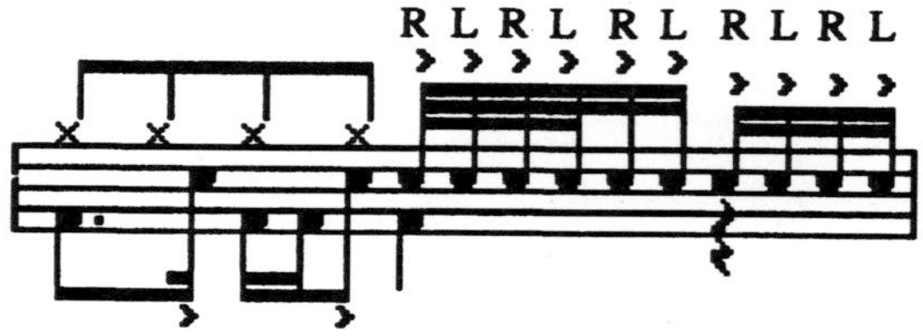

Measure 29

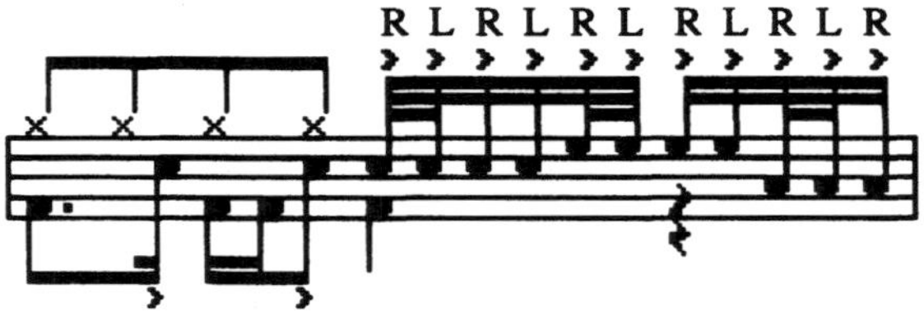

Measure 33

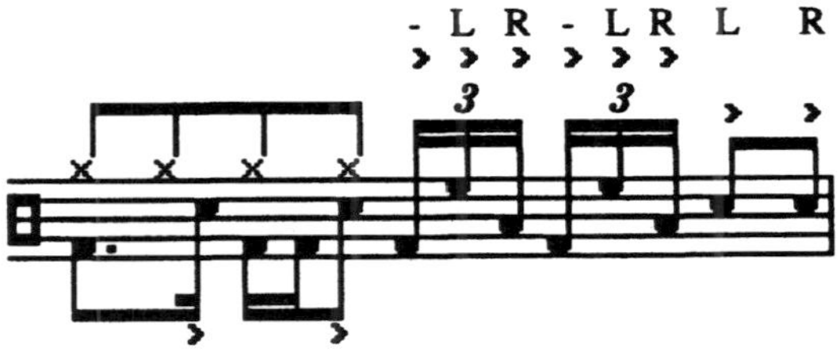

Measures 37–38

Chart Ten

Hard Rock

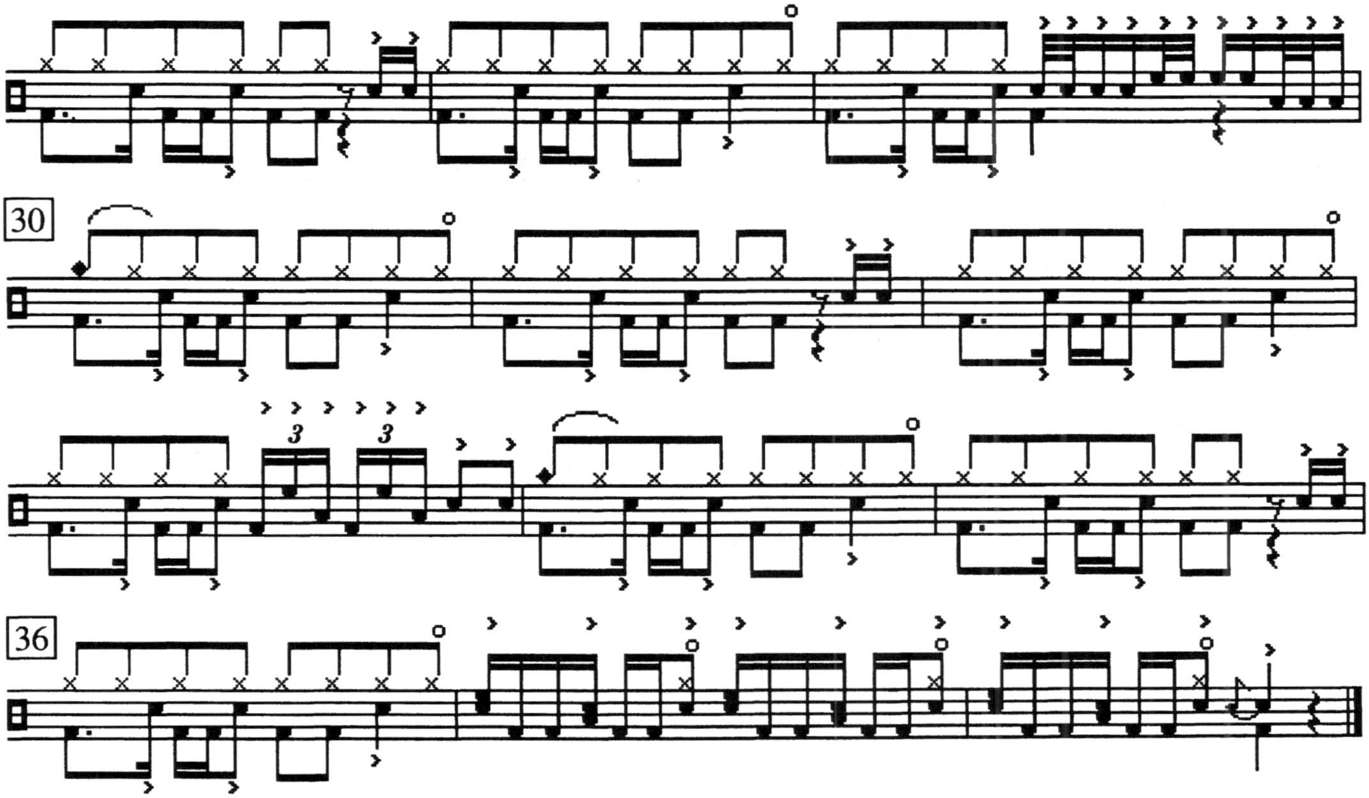
30
36

Other Books by James Morton

Easiest Drum Set Book

Fusion Drum Styles

Killer-Fillers for Drum Set

Rock Studies for Drum Set

You Can Teach Yourself® Drums